Blastoff! Missions takes you on a learning adventure! Colorful illustrations and exciting narratives highlight cool facts about our world and beyond. Read the mission goals and follow the narrative to gain knowledge, build reading skills, and have fun!

Traditional Nonfiction

Narrative Nonfiction

Blastoff! Universe

MISSION GOALS

> FIND YOUR SIGHT WORDS IN THE BOOK.

> LEARN ABOUT DIFFERENT PERIODS IN LONDON'S HISTORY.

> LEARN ABOUT DIFFERENT CHALLENGES LONDON HAS FACED.

This edition first published in 2024 by Bellwether Media, Inc.

No part of this publication may be reproduced in whole or in part without written permission of the publisher. For information regarding permission, write to Bellwether Media, Inc., Attention: Permissions Department, 6012 Blue Circle Drive, Minnetonka, MN 55343.

Library of Congress Cataloging-in-Publication Data

Names: Rathburn, Betsy, author. | Vaisberg, Diego, illustrator.
Title: London / by Betsy Rathburn ; illustrated by Diego Vaisberg.
Description: Minneapolis, MN : Bellwether Media, 2024. | Series: Blastoff! Missions: Cities Through Time | Includes bibliographical references and index. | Audience: Ages 5-8 | Audience: Grades 2-3 | Summary: "Vibrant illustrations accompany information about the history of London. The narrative nonfiction text is intended for students in kindergarten through third grade." - Provided by publisher.
Identifiers: LCCN 2023044997 (print) | LCCN 2023044998 (ebook) | ISBN 9798886877571 (library binding) | ISBN 9798886879452 (paperback) | ISBN 9798886378516 (ebook)
Subjects: LCSH: London (England)--History--Juvenile literature.
Classification: LCC DA678 .R38 2023 (print) | LCC DA678 (ebook) | DDC 942.1--dc23/eng/20230922
LC record available at https://lccn.loc.gov/2023044997
LC ebook record available at https://lccn.loc.gov/2023044998

Text copyright © 2024 by Bellwether Media, Inc. BLASTOFF! MISSIONS and associated logos are trademarks and/or registered trademarks of Bellwether Media, Inc.

Editor: Christina Leaf   Designer: Andrea Schneider

Printed in the United States of America, North Mankato, MN.

This is **Blastoff Jimmy**! He is here to help you on your mission and share fun facts along the way!

Table of Contents

Welcome to London!	4
Town to City	6
Growth and Change	14
The City Today	20
Glossary	22
To Learn More	23
Beyond the Mission	24
Index	24

Here we are in London, England! This capital city is home to around 9 million people. It is one of Europe's biggest cities. Let's explore its past!

Town to City

50 CE

Roman **invaders** built a new bridge. It is now easier to cross the River Thames.

They started a town by the bridge. Londinium will grow quickly!

River Thames

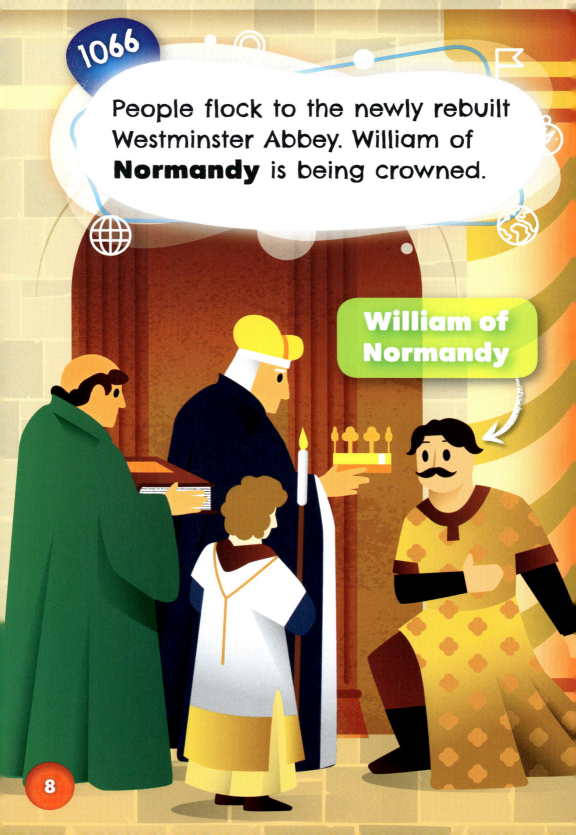

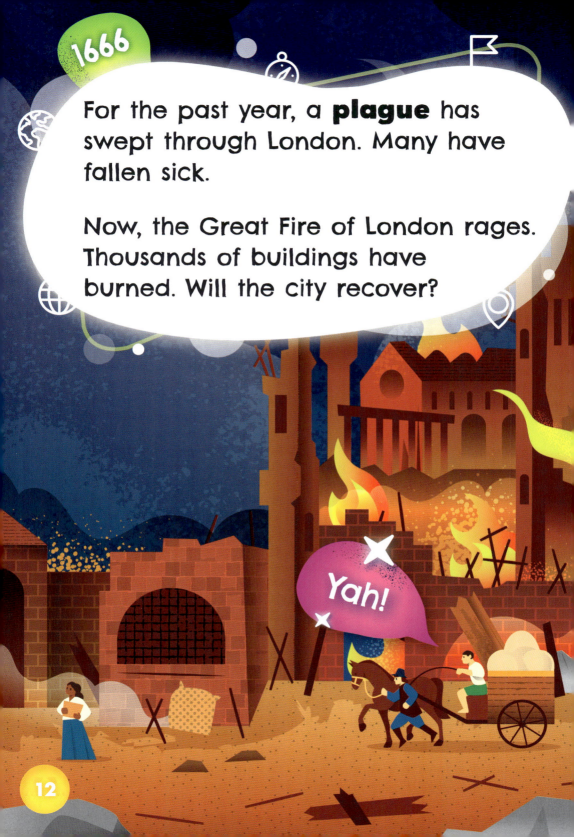

1666

For the past year, a **plague** has swept through London. Many have fallen sick.

Now, the Great Fire of London rages. Thousands of buildings have burned. Will the city recover?

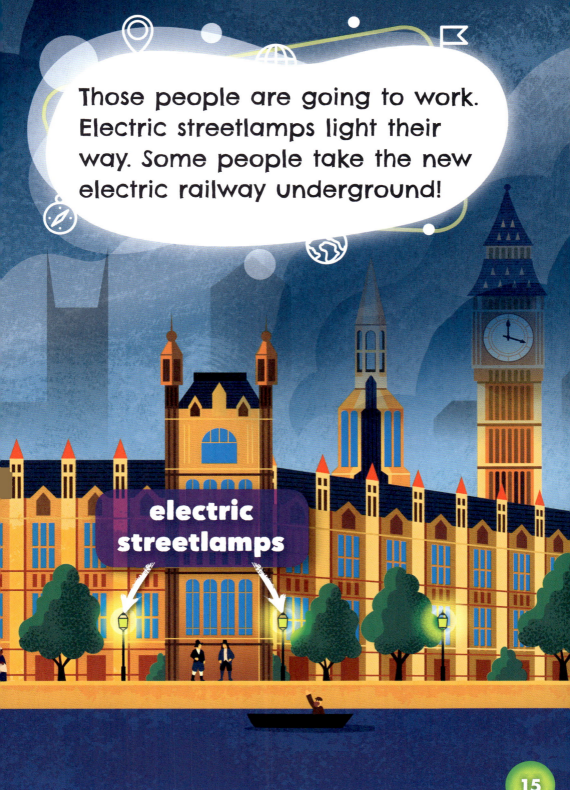

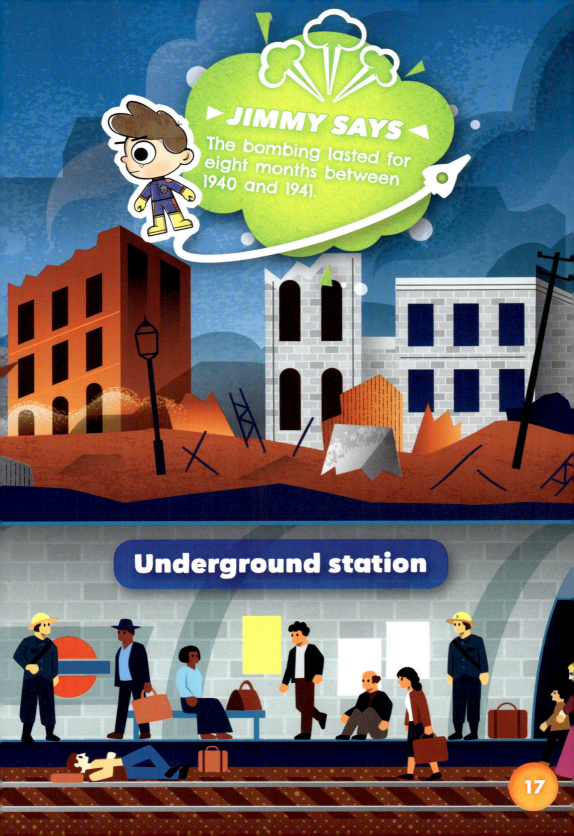

2023

Here comes King Charles III! His **coronation** at Westminster Abbey is the first in 70 years.

Now, he greets a crowd at Buckingham Palace. He is Britain's 62nd **monarch**!

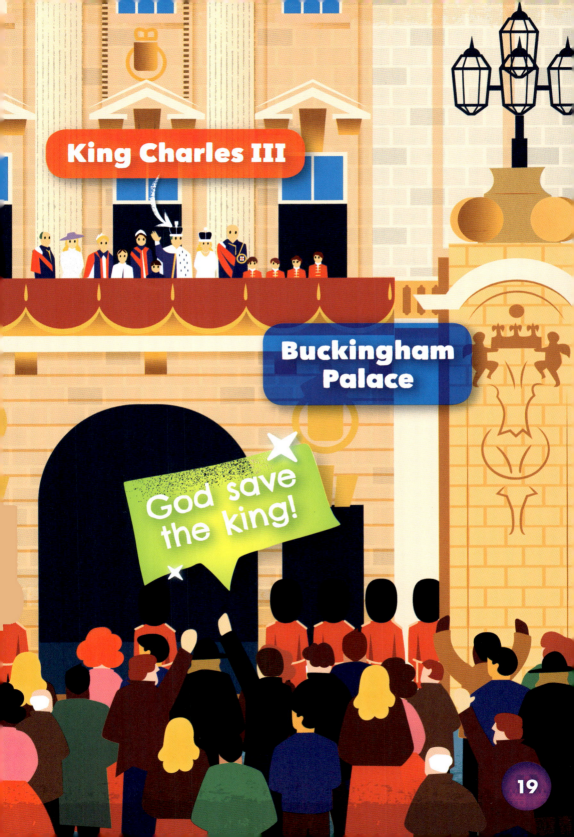

The City Today

today

Old and new buildings line London's streets. Grand bridges cross the River Thames. People head to historic theaters and new restaurants. London is a mix of **ancient** and **modern**!

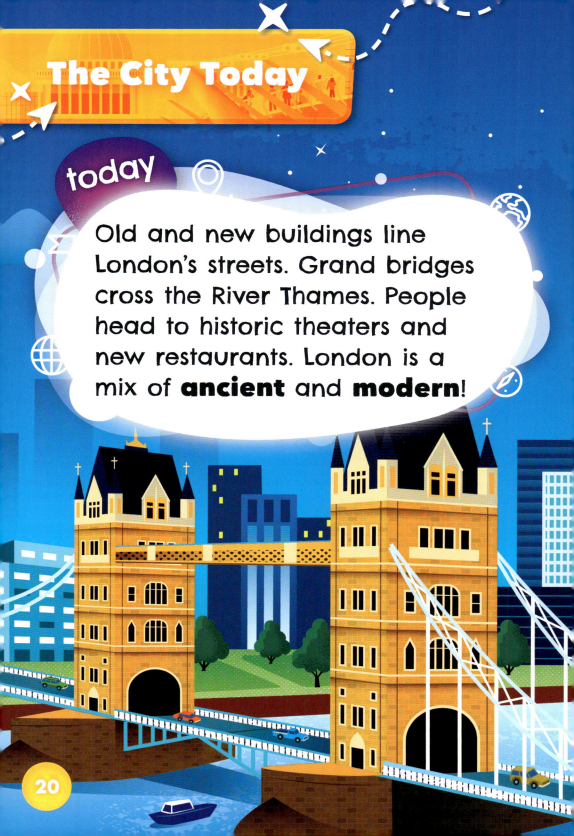

London Timeline

50 CE: The Roman town of Londinium grows around a bridge built over the River Thames

1066: William of Normandy becomes king of England

early 1600s: Many theater groups, including William Shakespeare's company, operate in London

1666: The Great Fire of London burns thousands of buildings

1890: The first electric railway opens in the London Underground

1940 to 1941: German planes drop bombs on London during World War II

2023: King Charles III is crowned

London, England

Glossary

ancient–from long ago

company–a group that puts on plays

coronation–an event during which a king or queen is crowned

industrial–having a lot of businesses that use machines to do work

invaders–people who come from one place to take over another place

modern–related to the present day

monarch–a person who rules

Normandy–a part of northern France

plague–a deadly disease that spreads quickly

playhouses–theaters

smog–fog and smoke that fill the air, often from factories

To Learn More

AT THE LIBRARY

Murray, Julie. *London Underground*. Minneapolis, Minn.: Abdo Zoom, 2022.

Roberts, Emma. *Shakespeare for Everyone: Discover the History, Comedy, and Tragedy of the World's Greatest Playwright*. London, U.K.: Magic Cat Publishing, 2022.

Sánchez Vegara, Maria Isabel. *King Charles*. London, U.K.: Frances Lincoln Children's Books, 2023.

ON THE WEB

FACTSURFER

Factsurfer.com gives you a safe, fun way to find more information.

1. Go to www.factsurfer.com.
2. Enter "London" into the search box and click 🔍.
3. Select your book cover to see a list of related content.

BEYOND THE MISSION

> WHAT FACT FROM THE BOOK DID YOU THINK WAS THE MOST INTERESTING?

> WHICH PART OF LONDON'S HISTORY WOULD YOU LIKE TO VISIT? WHY?

> DRAW A PICTURE OF A NEW BRIDGE TO CROSS THE RIVER THAMES.

Index

Battle of Hastings, 9
bombs, 16, 17
bridge, 6, 20
Buckingham Palace, 18
Charles III (king), 18, 19
coronation, 18
England, 5, 9
Europe, 5
factories, 14
Globe Theatre, 10, 11
Great Fire of London, 12
invaders, 6, 9
Londinium, 6, 7

monarch, 18
plague, 12
playhouses, 10
population, 5, 10
railway, 15
River Thames, 6, 20
Shakespeare, William, 11
smog, 14
streetlamps, 15
timeline, 21
Underground, 15, 16, 17
Westminster Abbey, 8, 18
William I (king), 8, 9

24